Easy-to-give
OBJECT
LESSONS

by

Charles C. Ryrie

moody press
chicago

Introduction

SUGGESTIONS FOR THE USE OF OBJECT LESSONS

Object lessons are God's own idea (1 Corinthians 10:11), so we do well to use them. The use of an illustration is not only a good way to convey the meaning of scriptural truth, sometimes it is the only way (see Romans 9:20-22). But the illustration should be common, for the sake of the pupil's remembering, and simple, for the sake of the teacher's preparing.

Every effort has been made to keep these object lessons simple, but they are not complete. The teacher is encouraged to take the seed thoughts contained in these pages, nurture them in his or her own heart, and then present them to the class. In this way, under the guidance of the Holy Spirit, the lesson will become his own and the message will be the Lord's message for that particular occasion. Even as canned food must be warmed and served attractively, so prepared lessons must be warmed in the teacher's heart and served to the class with careful preparation.

May the One who said, "Suffer little children to come unto me," be pleased to use these object lessons to win to Himself these children, "for of such is the kingdom of heaven" (Matthew 19:14).

CHARLES C. RYRIE

© 1974 by
THE MOODY BIBLE INSTITUTE
OF CHICAGO

Selected object lessons included in this book have been compiled from volumes 1-4 of *Easy-to-Get Object Lessons* by Charles Ryrie (Grand Rapids: Zondervan, 1949-).

ISBN: 0-8024-2291-8

Second Printing, 1975

Library of Congress Catalog Card Number: 74-15335

Printed in the United States of America

Contents

LESSON   PAGE

    Introduction

LESSONS FOR EVANGELISM

1.	A Plane Ticket	5
2.	Faith	6
3.	My Diary	7
4.	The Right Combination	8
5.	A Gift for You	9
6.	Black Paint	10
7.	A Rubber Band	11
8.	The True Picture	12
9.	The Lost Pen	13
10.	The Broom	14
11.	Something I made	15
12.	A Prescription	16
13.	A Peanut	17
14.	Proofs of Life	18
15.	Counterfeits	19
16.	Something Enduring	20
17.	"Be Ye Ready"	21
18.	Windows	22
19.	All Dressed Up	23
20.	A Dirty Cup	24

LESSONS FOR THE CHRISTIAN LIFE

21.	A Milk Bottle	25
22.	Not Yours	26
23.	All to Him	27
24.	The Light of the World	28
25.	My Heart	29

26.	An Onion	30
27.	Fish, Salt, and You	31
28.	Salt	32
29.	Keeping Warm	33
30.	Growing Up	34
31.	A Piece of Bread	35
32.	A Loaf of Bread	36
33.	Hypocrisy	37
34.	Like a Diamond	38
35.	Special Delivery	39
36.	Fifth-Amendment Christians	40
37.	The Finished Product	41
38.	Tearing Down or Building Up?	42
39.	Filled and Used	43
40.	Strength and Unity	44
41.	Light Bulbs	45
42.	Walking	46
43.	The Temperature	47
44.	The Importance of Today	48
45.	Heaven	49
46.	A Flashlight	50
47.	A Compass	51
48.	My Glasses	52
49.	Ask the Author	53
50.	A Mirror	54
51.	Stopped Watches	55
52.	Worship	56
53.	Time Is Running Out	57
54.	Water, Water Everywhere	58
55.	Mind Your Mind	59
56.	On Growing Up	60
57.	Joined Together	61
58.	My Aching Foot	62
59.	On Communion Sunday	63
60.	On Easter	64

1

A Plane Ticket

OBJECT: A plane ticket, or any transportation ticket, even a bus transfer.

LESSON: Jesus Christ is the only way to the Father (John 14:6).

PRESENTATION: You see that I have here a ticket that will let me ride from Dallas to St. Louis. (*Substitute names to fit the local situation.*) Very soon I'm going to use the ticket, and when I get on the plane and hand it to the stewardess, it will take me all the way to St. Louis, where I'm going to see my father.

I have another ticket here today, too, but it's in my heart; that ticket is the Lord Jesus Christ. I took Him by faith, and He's going to take me all the way to heaven, where I'm going to see my heavenly Father. This plane ticket is all paid for. That's also true of the ticket in my heart. It's all paid for, but at an awful price. Jesus Christ, the Son of God, had to die in order that I, by taking Him as Saviour, might get to heaven.

Since I have this ticket to St. Louis, I'd be very foolish not to use it, wouldn't I? Suppose that on the day I planned to leave, you saw me out at the airport and I started to run along the runway to St. Louis. How far do you think I'd get? I doubt if I would get very far! And yet there are many, many people who are trying to get to heaven by their own efforts. How far do you think they're going to get?

Now, this ticket has a date on it, and I can't use it after that date. Boys and girls, soon the Lord Jesus is coming again, and if you don't have a ticket to heaven in your heart, it will be too late. Is He your Saviour today? If not, accept Him now.

2

Faith

OBJECT: A nickel.

LESSON: Faith is necessary to salvation (Ephesians 2:8-9).

PRESENTATION: The first boy or girl who comes up here will get this nickel. (*Hold up clenched fist with nickel in it but do not show it. The offer will probably have to be repeated.*) Here comes someone. Let me ask you, do you really believe that I have a nickel here, and do you really believe that I am going to give it to you? Well, you're right. I have a nickel in my hand, and I said that the first one to come would receive it. Since you believed me, you are going to get the nickel.

Do you know what that illustrates? Faith. In this case, faith means simply believing that what I said was true. Do you boys and girls know that Jesus Christ said that not the first one only but anyone and everyone who comes to Him for eternal life will receive it if he will believe in Him? If you have never accepted by faith the Lord Jesus Christ as your own Saviour from sin, will you go to Him and do it today?

Our little friend had to come for this nickel himself. Just so, you must take Jesus Christ for yourself. No one can do it for you. Now, here's your nickel, just as I promised. You didn't have to work for it, did you? And you can't work for salvation either (Ephesians 2:8-9). If you are unsaved, trust Jesus Christ, and He will save you. Let's bow our heads while those who would like to be saved go to Him now in prayer and tell Him that they take Him as their Saviour.

3

My Diary

OBJECT: A diary.

LESSON: Your name should be written in the book of life (Revelation 13:8).

PRESENTATION: Today I have my diary with me. Do you know what I keep in my diary? Well, I write many things in it: important events, and interesting things that have happened. I'm going to read a few things to you now. Listen. "July 23—Billy accepted Christ as Saviour today. . . . September 6—Two were saved in Sunday school today."

Did you know that God keeps a dairy? Do you know what He calls His diary? Well, He calls it the "Book of Life." And do you know what He writes in His diary? He writes the name of everyone who is saved—that is, everyone who has received by faith Jesus Christ as his very own personal Saviour.

It doesn't make much difference whether or not your name is in my diary, but it is very important that your name be written in God's diary, the Book of Life. I may lose my diary, but God never loses His. The ink may fade so that you will not be able to read my diary, but that will never happen to God's diary. I may forget to include your name in my diary, but God never forgets.

Oh, if your name isn't in that Book of Life, it can be today if you will only accept God's gift of His Son as your own Saviour now. The moment you do that, you will be saved for all eternity, and God will write your name in the Book of Life. If you've never done it, accept Christ now.

4

The Right Combination

OBJECT: A combination lock.

LESSON: The way of salvation is Jesus Christ (Acts 16:31).

PRESENTATION: Here's a combination lock that we're going to try to open today, and we're going to let it represent all unsaved people who are bound by sin. I have a bunch of keys here and we could try to use them on this lock. Do you think they will work? Of course not.

Well, suppose you try to open it. (*Hand it to someone.*) You can't do it? (*Hand it to someone else.*) Well, you try. We don't seem to be making much progress getting this lock open. Let's see if we can do better in working something out to free the unsaved person from his sin. Will the combination of good works do it? No, for the Bible says, "Not by works of righteousness which we have done" (Titus 3:5). Let's try baptism. Will that wash away sins? No, of course not.

I have a piece of paper here with the combination of this lock on it. Do you suppose that if I tried that combination it would open? Well, let's see. (*Open lock.*) There, you see that it works. I also have a Book here which tells me how a sinner can be loosed from his sins. It says, "Believe on the Lord Jesus Christ, and thou shalt be saved" (Acts 16:31). Does that work? Yes, for God has said that it would, and those of us who have believed know that it does.

Is there any other combination that will work this lock? No, and there's no other way to be saved, for the Bible says, "There is none other name under heaven given among men, whereby we must be saved" (Acts 4:12). Could I add to or subtract from this combination and expect it to work? No, and you cannot add anything to what Christ has done for you by dying for your sins. All you have to do to be freed from your sins is to accept right now what He has done for you.

5

A Gift for You

OBJECT: A watch or other valuable article.

LESSON: Salvation is a gift (Romans 6:23).

PRESENTATION: You see this watch that I have here today. Would you like to have it? (*Offer it to someone.*) All right, I here and now give it to you. (*Keep the object in your hand, however.*) Have you got it? Of course not. Well, why not? I certainly gave it to you. There's nothing more that I can do. The reason you don't have it is that you haven't taken it, isn't it? How are you going to get it? Simply by taking it. All right, now take it. Do you have it now?

Boys and girls, salvation is a gift, and God is saying to you today, if you aren't already saved, "Here is the gift of My Son; do you want Him as your Saviour?" There's nothing more that God can do than that which He has already done, for He gave His only Son to die on Calvary's cross for your sins, and He offers salvation to you freely.

There's nothing you can do to earn salvation. The question is simply: Do you have Jesus Christ in your heart? If not, just as all you had to do to get this watch was to take it, so all you have to do to be saved is to take Jesus Christ by faith as your own personal Saviour. Would you like to have God's gift? All right, reach out to God and accept by faith the gift of His Son as your very own.

9

6

Black Paint

OBJECT: A bottle of turpentine; black paint on the tip of one finger.

LESSON: Only the blood of Christ can remove sin (1 John 1:7b).

PRESENTATION: The other day I was painting, and I got some paint on my finger, just as I have today. We're going to let this paint represent sin; everyone born into this world has a sinful heart, for all have sinned, the Bible says (Romans 3:23). The problem is how to get rid of this sin.

Well, there are some people who try to cover it up like this. (Close hand tightly.) You can plainly see what happens—it spreads. (Paint will be on the palm of the hand when it is opened.) If I should scratch my face, I would get paint all over my face. You cannot cover up sin from the sight of others, and certainly not from the sight of God. What can we do?

The other day when I was painting, the first thing I did after I finished was to try to wash off the paint. I should have known better, because the paint did not come off at all. By your own efforts you won't be able to wash away your sin. People try to do so in many different ways but they all fail. Some are baptized, some join a church, and some do many good works, but that awful stain of sin still remains.

Let's try this bottle of turpentine. You see what is happening—the paint is coming off, and I don't even have to scrub it. Just so, there is only one way to remove that stain of sin, and that way is by the blood of Jesus Christ, which was shed for you on Calvary's cross. You don't have to do anything. Simply accept Jesus Christ as your personal Saviour, and His precious blood will cleanse your heart. Do it right now if you've never done it.

7

A Rubber Band

OBJECT: A rubber band.

LESSON: God's promises and longsuffering are certain (2 Peter 3:9).

PRESENTATION: Some people say that we Christians are mistaken to expect that the Lord will return. They say that He has been away so long that we can never expect Him to return. But the Bible says that He surely will return (1 Thessalonians 4:13-18), and it also says that "the Lord is not slack concerning his promise, as some men count slackness; but is longsuffering to us-ward, not willing that any should perish, but that all should come to repentance" (2 Peter 3:9).

Look at this rubber band for a moment. Just as sure as I know that the Lord is going to come, so I know that this rubber band will break if I stretch it enough. Now, I can stretch this rubber band quite a bit before it will break. This verse that I just read said that the Lord is longsuffering, and His patience has been stretched much longer than this rubber band, for the Lord has delayed His coming for almost two thousand years. Rubber bands can be stretched so that they go around larger and larger bundles. That's just the reason the Lord has delayed His coming—so that more people can be saved.

Perhaps there are some here who have put off being saved. Don't put it off any longer, because someday, in the twinkling of an eye, He is going to come. When the last person that is going to be saved is saved, the Lord will come. (*Stretch the band until it breaks.*) Then it will be too late. But it's not too late now if you will accept Jesus Christ as your Saviour today. "Behold, now is the accepted time; behold, now is the day of salvation" (2 Corinthians 6:2).

8

The True Picture

OBJECT: A mirror and a retouched photograph of yourself, if possible.

LESSON: All have sinned, but all may be saved (Romans 3:23; 6:23).

PRESENTATION: When you go to a photographer and have your picture taken, before he delivers the finished product to you he does what is known as "retouching." Some pictures require more retouching than others, of course. Now, there are some people in the world who like to retouch what the Bible says, but the Bible is like a mirror, for it sees us exactly as we are.

Sometimes it's not pleasant for us to look in the mirror, especially when we're dirty. We would rather try to fool ourselves. But when it comes to eternal things and questions about sin and salvation, we had better not try to fool ourselves, for we could make a terrible mistake. Now let's see what the Bible says about these things.

First we read, "all have sinned, and come short of the glory of God" (Romans 3:23). Then we also read that "the wages of sin is death" (Romans 6:23). If we stopped there it wouldn't be a very pretty picture, but the Bible goes on to say that "the gift of God is eternal life through Jesus Christ our Lord" (Romans 6:23). All you have to do to be saved from sin is to accept that gift, which is Jesus Christ, as your personal Saviour. God is in the business of saving sinners. Don't try to retouch the picture the Bible gives. If you recognize yourself as a sinner needing a Saviour, accept the Lord Jesus today.

9

The Lost Pen

OBJECT: A fountain pen or a pencil hidden in the inside coat pocket of a man's coat or in a woman's pocketbook.

LESSON: The unsaved are lost, and Christians must work to win them (2 Peter 3:9).

PRESENTATION: Somehow I seem to have lost my fountain pen, and I can't find it anywhere. Since this has happened, let's use it for an object lesson and let this lost pen represent every unsaved person, because every unsaved person is lost, too.

I am really very fond of my pen and I want very much to find it, just as God wants lost sinners to be saved, for He has said that He is "not willing that any should perish, but that all should come to repentance" (2 Peter 3:9). Now, it's certain that if this pen is going to be found I'm going to have to do it. It surely can't find itself. And if you're not a Christian, you can't save yourself. Someone has to do it, and the Lord Jesus Christ is that Person.

Let's see if I can find my pen. Yes, here it is, way down in my inside coat pocket. It's very dark down there, but every unbeliever is in darkness many times darker than that in this pocket. Why was I so interested in finding this pen? Because I like it and I want to use it. And God wants to use every Christian to His own glory. He won't force you, but if you will let Him, He will use you. So, if you have never trusted Christ as Saviour, do that right now. And if you have already trusted Him as your Saviour, give Him your life so that He can use you.

10

The Broom

OBJECT: A broom.

LESSON: Self-reformation is worthless (Matthew 12:43-45).

PRESENTATION: I expect that all of you know what this is and what it is used for. There are in the world today many unsaved people who are trying to use the broom of self-reformation on their own lives. They think that if they clean their lives, they will somehow get to heaven. There are also people who will tell you that they will accept Christ as soon as they stop doing certain things in their lives. They think that they have to be very good people before they can be saved.

When the Lord Jesus was here on earth, He told a story about such people. (*Read Matthew* 12:43-45.) You see that this man got rid of his evil habits, swept his house, and thought he was secure. But what happened? The old habits returned, and even more wicked ones came with them, and the last state of that man was worse than the first. You see, he tried by his own efforts to get rid of his sin, and he failed.

If you're burdened today with a load of sin, quit trying to clean yourself, and let Jesus Christ save you from sin. When He does the work, He creates in you an entirely new nature (2 Corinthians 5:17). Christ came to save sinners; realize that today and cast yourself on Him. He says, "Come unto me, all ye that labour and are heavy laden, and I will give you rest" (Matthew 11:28).

11

Something I Made

OBJECT: Anything you yourself have made. A simple drawing will suffice.

LESSON: Everyone must face his Creator.

PRESENTATION: Do you know where I got the object I am using today? I made it. Since it is mine, I have the right to do anything I want to do with it. If I wish to tear it up, you have no right to protest, because I am the creator.

God created each of you boys and girls, and someday each of you will have to meet your Creator. For some it will be a wonderful occasion; for others, a terrible time of judgment. Which will it be for you?

If you're not sure, let me tell you how you can be saved from judgment. God doesn't want to condemn any of you. He wants to save you, and He wants to do this so much that He sent His Son, the Lord Jesus Christ, to this earth to die for your sins. God must judge sin, but Christ paid for your sins on the cross, and He will take your sin away right now if you will take Him into your heart. If your sins have been taken away, you can meet your Creator unafraid. Will you let the Lord Jesus Christ come into your heart and take away your sin?

12

A Prescription

OBJECT: A prescription for medicine.

LESSON: Christ is the cure for sin (Acts 16:31).

PRESENTATION: Not so long ago, I was sick. I don't like to be sick, so I went to the doctor to see if he could do something to help me. After looking me over, he gave me this medicine to take, and he told me that if I would take it I would get well. I have faith in my doctor, and I believed that if I took the medicine I would get well. So I took it and I recovered.

Boys and girls, everyone born into this world has the disease of sin, and everyone would die from this disease if nothing were done for him. But there's a Doctor who can cure this disease. He's the Great Physician, and He's the only One who can help sin-sick people. God tells us in His Word that if we believe on the Lord Jesus Christ as our very own Saviour from our sin, we will be saved from this horrible thing. "Believe on the Lord Jesus Christ, and thou shalt be saved, and thy house" (Acts 16:31). Now, if you will believe what God says, and take, not medicine as I have here, but a Person, Jesus Christ, as your Saviour, God will forgive you all your sins. That's simple, isn't it?

Suppose I had bought this medicine and, knowing that it could cure me, I had refused to take it. You'd think that was foolish, wouldn't you? And yet some of you here today are refusing to take Jesus Christ as your Saviour, even though He is the only cure and even though He has paid for your salvation by dying for your sins. Why refuse Him any longer? Why not accept Him today? Bow your head now, and tell the Saviour that you believe that He died for you and that you want Him to save you from sin.

13

A Peanut

OBJECT: An unshelled peanut.

LESSON: The way of salvation is through faith.

PRESENTATION: You all know what this is. It's a peanut. But has anyone of you ever seen the nut that's inside? How do you know it's there? Well, there are two ways that you can know. First of all, you can take my word for it that there is a nut inside this shell. You see, I've shaken it and I can hear that there's a nut inside. Then, secondly, since all of you have seen other peanuts, you know that they have nuts in them and of course you assume, and quite rightly, that there is a nut in this shell.

Now, boys and girls, this peanut illustrates salvation. You've never seen salvation, so how do you know that there is such a thing? For the same two reasons that you know the peanut is inside the shell. First of all, you have God's Word. He says that if you simply believe that Jesus Christ died for your sins, He will give you salvation. God is never wrong, and He never goes back on His word.

All of you have seen that trusting Christ as Saviour works in other people's lives, and consequently it follows that believing on Him will work in your life, too. So if there is anyone here who has never accepted Jesus Christ as his or her very own Saviour, do it right now. Other people have tried it and know that it works. But what's more important than that—God has said He will guarantee that salvation will be yours the moment you accept the Lord Jesus as your Saviour. Will you trust Him now?

14

Proofs of Life

OBJECT: A young child.

LESSON: There should be evidence of the new life in the Christian.

PRESENTATION: I want one of you to be the object today. Our object looks very much alive, doesn't he? Well, he is alive, but if he were lying down with his eyes closed, it would perhaps be very difficult to tell that he was alive. But I want to show you how you can tell that he has life.

First of all, you saw the object get up and walk to the front. In other words, he acts very much alive. Now, boys and girls, there are many people who say that they are Christians, but they do not act like Christians. The Bible tells us that Christians ought to walk differently when they are saved (1 John 2:6); so if they do not, then we may doubt that they are alive spiritually. If the object here didn't move at all, you would wonder if he were alive; and if you aren't living as a Christian should, then perhaps you do not have eternal life.

We also know that the object is alive because he talks. Just so, Christians talk for their Lord and Saviour. It makes no difference how young you are, if you are saved you should be talking for the Lord Jesus Christ. When the object opens his mouth he lets people know that he is alive, and if you are a Christian, you should let everyone know that you are a follower of the Lord Jesus. This means that many things have no place in the Christian's conversation.

What about it? Do you have life that comes from God? If you are not walking and talking as a Christian should, then maybe you were never really saved. So if you are not sure, or if you want to be saved, accept the Lord Jesus Christ as your Saviour from sin right now where you are.

18

15

Counterfeits

OBJECT: An imitation diamond ring and a real one, or a counterfeit coin and a real one of the same denomination.

LESSON: There is a difference between real and professing Christians (James 2:20*b*).

PRESENTATION: You can see that I have two rings here today. They are very good-looking rings, and they both look like real diamonds. We're going to let these represent two people who *say* they are Christians. But I'll let you in on a little secret—one of these rings came from the dime store and of course is not real at all, although the other one is a real diamond. Just so, there are many people in the world today who say they are Christians but who really are not.

The question is, How are we going to tell which of these rings is real and which is the imitation? The mountings aren't the same, but to us the stones themselves look exactly alike. If I were a jeweler, I could tell which of these rings is the genuine one by looking through one of those glasses that jewelers have. And, boys and girls, God knows which of you are really genuinely saved, for Christ said, "I . . . know my sheep, and am known of mine" (John 10:14).

But there is another way we could find out about these rings. We could see which one would cut through a window, for the diamond would cut glass and the glass ring would be ruined. (*If a coin is used, indicate the fact that a counterfeit coin will not ring.*) Now, the Bible says that real Christians will be known by their good works, for James tells us that faith without works is dead, and if you aren't showing forth good works, then perhaps you are not a real Christian. So if you've never been saved, or if you're not sure you are saved, then be sure of it today by accepting Jesus Christ as your own personal Saviour.

19

16

Something Enduring

OBJECT: A faded flower and a bit of dry grass.

LESSON: The Word of God is abiding and true (Isaiah 40:7-8).

PRESENTATION: Look at this flower. What has happened to it? It's faded, isn't it? Look at this grass. It's withered and dry, isn't it? Look at my shoes. Look at that bush outside. Look at the chairs. Everything around us is passing away.

But do you know that there is one thing that endures forever and never passes away or wears out? Listen to these verses from the Bible: "The grass withereth, the flower fadeth: because the spirit of the LORD bloweth upon it: surely the people is grass. The grass withereth, the flower fadeth: but the word of our God shall stand for ever" (Isaiah 40:7-8). People spend hours and hours raising flowers that fade in a little while, and they spend a great deal of time trying to grow beautiful grass; yet how much time do they—do you—spend reading and studying God's Word, which never passes away?

It is true that flowers look pretty for a while, but after a short time they are no good at all. But this is not true of God's Word. It has been good throughout hundreds of years and it is still true today. One of the truths of the Word of God is this: if you will accept the Lord Jesus Christ as your own Saviour, He will save you from your sins. All God asks of you is to believe that the Lord Jesus died for you. Are you saved today? If not, take God at His word, for His word endures forever.

17

"Be Ye Ready"

OBJECT: A calendar.

LESSON: We do not know when the return of our Lord will occur.

PRESENTATION: I expect that all of you use a calendar rather often. Who can tell me what a calendar is used for? Yes, it tells us where we are with respect to time, and it also points out special, important days. Now, God has a calendar—the Bible— and the next important event on God's calendar is the return of the Lord Jesus Christ.

This calendar that I have here will tell me exactly when Easter occurs, for instance. But God's calendar has not told us when the Lord is going to come again. As a matter of fact, the Bible says just the opposite, for we read, "Of that day and hour knoweth no man" (Matthew 24:36).

When some special holiday is drawing near, we are reminded in many ways that it is near, and we are urged to make ready for it. At Christmastime, for instance, we buy presents and send out cards. God is reminding us in various ways that the coming of the Lord is very near, and He urges us in His Word to be prepared for it. Matthew tells us, "Therefore be ye also ready" (24:44), and John says, "And every man that hath this hope in him purifieth himself, even as he is pure" (1 John 3:3).

When the Lord comes, will you be ready? Of course, if you are not saved, you must accept the Lord Jesus as your Saviour before you can be ready. But if you are saved, you must live a pure life, so that when the Lord comes He won't find you doing something you ought not to be doing. So let's remember that any day on this calendar may be the day of the Lord's coming, and let's be ready for Him.

18

Windows

OBJECT: A window.

LESSON: The Christian needs constant cleansing (1 John 1:9).

PRESENTATION: When that window was first put in, it was very dirty, and someone had to clean it. It couldn't clean itself; someone had to do it. Just so, every person born into this world is dirty with sin, and the only way he or she can be cleansed from sin is to be washed in the blood of Jesus Christ by simply accepting Him as Saviour.

How many of you have ever broken a window? You know that you can't patch it so that Mother and Dad won't discover it. You yourself can't patch your sin-wrecked life, either, but Jesus Christ, if He is your Saviour, can do more than patch it. He will give you new life. The Bible says that "if any man be in Christ, he is a new creature" (2 Corinthians 5:17). If you want new life, accept Jesus Christ as your Saviour.

These windows keep getting dirty, and they need to be washed again and again. How many of you have ever washed windows for Mother? Well, Christians need to clean themselves, too. The Bible says that this should be done "with the washing of water by the word" (Ephesians 5:26). This means that you should read the Bible every day and let it point out to you the sin in your life. Then confess that sin to God, and He will cleanse you (1 John 1:9).

When windows get dirty, you can't see out of them, can you? Well, when your lives get dirty with sin—and I'm speaking to Christians now—others can't see Christ in you, so Christians should remember to keep clean by reading the Bible. If you've never been cleansed by the blood of Christ, accept Him now as your Saviour.

19

All Dressed Up

OBJECT: You or some child.

LESSON: Be prepared for the Lord's coming.

PRESENTATION: Come up here a minute, will you, Johnny? My, but you're certainly dressed up this morning. Look at that nice suit, and those beautiful new shoes. You hair is all combed, and you're really fixed up. Why is it you're so dressed up this morning? Oh, it's because you know you were coming to Sunday school and church. Do you mean to tell me that you don't usually wear these clothes to school and out to play? Of course not.

Well, tell me, why didn't you put your play clothes on this morning? You surely did yesterday, didn't you? Certainly, you knew that today was Sunday and you prepared for it. You didn't get all dressed up today because you are going to church tomorrow, did you? Of course not. You got dressed up because you were coming to church today.

Suppose, boys and girls, you knew that Jesus was coming back to earth today. Would it make any difference how you acted today? Would you live differently this afternoon if you knew Jesus was coming back tonight? Well, the Bible teaches us that He might come today. How, then, should you be living? If you really expect the Lord to come today, you'll be ready for Him, just like Johnny expected to come to church today and got all dressed up for the occasion. How can you be prepared for the Lord's coming? Well, you must have all sin in your life confessed and forgiven by Him. If you've done something wrong this week, then right now, bow your head, and ask Him to forgive you. Then you will be ready if He comes today.

20

A Dirty Cup

OBJECT: A cup that is clean on the outside but dirty on the inside.

LESSON: We should not be hypocrites.

PRESENTATION: How would you like a nice, cool drink from this cup? Do you really think you would? It is a nice cup, isn't it? And it does look clean. But I've only shown you the outside. Look at the inside. Now, nobody wants a drink.

The Lord Jesus said something about dirty cups and plates. Talking to the Pharisees He said, "Ye make clean the outside of the cup and of the platter, but within they are full of extortion and excess. Thou blind Pharisee, cleanse first that which is within the cup and platter, that the outside of them may be clean also" (Matthew 23:25-26). The Lord was speaking against hypocrisy—that is, against people who are outwardly one thing and inwardly another. And the Lord spoke very strongly and harshly against that sin, for He hates it.

Suppose we apply this illustration to ourselves. This cup is like the boy or girl who acts very nice sometimes, who may even know all the answers to questions about God, the Bible, and Jesus, but who on the inside has never had his or her heart cleansed from sin. Some are even fooled into thinking that such a person is a Christian because no one but God can look into a person's heart and see what is there. But God can, and does.

God knows, and so do you. Is your heart clean today? Have you had your sins completely washed away? Is Jesus your Saviour from all sin?

21

A Milk Bottle

OBJECT: A milk bottle.

LESSON: Our Lord desires surrendered lives (1 Corinthians 6:19-20).

PRESENTATION: Today I have a very common object. It's just a plain, ordinary milk bottle. We're going to let it represent every true Christian—that is, everyone who has accepted Jesus Christ as Saviour. To whom does this milk bottle belong? It doesn't belong to me, but to the dairy from which I bought the milk. If you're saved, you don't belong to yourself any more, for the Bible says that "ye are not your own" (1 Corinthians 6:19).

Do I have any right to keep this bottle? Many people keep milk bottles longer than they should, and many Christians keep their lives for themselves when they have no right to do so. They belong to the Lord and He should be the One to direct them. When I bought this quart of milk I had to pay the grocer more than the milk cost. I paid him a deposit on the bottle so I would remember that it wasn't mine but that it belonged to him. The Bible says that "ye are bought with a price" (1 Corinthians 6:20), and that price wasn't money, but it was the precious blood of the Lord Jesus who died for you. In view of the awful price He had to pay for us, ought not we to give back to Him our lives which rightfully belong to Him?

If I want any more milk in this bottle, I will have to take it back to the milkman and let him fill it. Likewise, if you want joy and happiness and fruit in your Christian life, you will have to give it back to Christ so that He can fill you and use you for His own glory.

25

22

Not Yours

OBJECT: A pencil imprinted with someone's name.

LESSON: "You are not your own, for you are bought with a price" (1 Corinthians 6:19-20).

PRESENTATION: Look at this pencil I have today. Do you see what's special about it? Yes, that's right, it has a person's name printed on it right here where you normally see the brand name stamped. Do you see whose name it is? That's right, this pencil belongs to my daughter, Carolyn. There's her name stamped right on it. How many of you have pencils or pens with your name on them?

Now let me ask you a question which has a very obvious answer. Whose pencil is this? Why, Carolyn's, of course. It's not mine; it's not yours; it's hers. And how do you know? Because her name is on the pencil.

Let me ask you another question. If you are a child of God, to whom do you belong? If Jesus Christ is your Saviour, to whom do you belong? The answer is just obvious, isn't it? You belong to Christ. How do you know? Because you are a Christian—you have His name.

How do you get a pencil like this? Well, you send some money in to some company, and the company prints your name on the pencil. It costs something to have this done. Just so, it costs something for you to be able to be a Christian and bear the name of Christ in your life. Imprinted pencils don't cost very much, but Christians have been bought with the blood of Christ. It cost the Lord Jesus His life in order that you and I may be called Christians.

What do you think I should do with this pencil. Throw it away? Of course not. I must give it right back to Carolyn because it's hers. I must not keep it. Likewise, if you are a Christian, your life belongs to Christ. Don't throw it away on selfish ambitions. Give it back to Christ, to whom it really belongs.

23

All to Him

OBJECT: The imprinted pencil used in the previous lesson.

LESSON: It is foolish not to give all to Christ.

PRESENTATION: Do you remember the pencil I had last week with Carolyn's name imprinted on it? I hope you remember the lesson—since we have been purchased by the blood of Christ, we belong to Him.

Now, this pencil belongs to Carolyn, and that's quite obvious since there's her name on it as plain as day. Who should have this pencil then? Carolyn, of course. But I have it. As a matter of fact, I've had it in my possession all week. That's not right, is it? And furthermore, I've been using the pencil, too.

I know Carolyn wants her pencil back, because she asked me for it after the lesson last week. But I haven't given it to her. Actually, I rather like her pencil. It writes well. It's still pretty long so there's lots of use left in it. The eraser is still quite good. I think I'll keep it. But Carolyn wants it, and it is hers.

What shall I do? I know. There's a way we can both be satisfied. I'll just break the pencil in two (break it in front of the children). I'll give her one of these pieces and keep the other. She should be satisfied now, shouldn't she? But, you say, she won't like that. Well, suppose I give her the half that has the eraser on it. That certainly should make her happy (and me too, because I still have part to use). But, you insist, it isn't right. The whole pencil is hers, and actually by breaking it, I have practically ruined it. I should have given it all to her in the first place.

Do you see the point? The Lord wants all of us, not just some part of our lives or time or energy or money that may be convenient to give Him. If we try to break off part for ourselves, we'll just make a mess of things. Everything we have belongs to Him. We belong to him. Let's give ourselves completely to Him.

24

The Light of the World

OBJECT: A clock or watch with a radium dial.

LESSON: We need constant fellowship with the Lord.

PRESENTATION: What's very special about this clock that I have today? Yes, it has radium on the face so that you can see it in the dark. We're going to let this represent every Christian boy and girl. The Lord Jesus Christ said, "Ye are the light of the world" (Matthew 5:14). But our Lord also said that He Himself was the Light of the world (John 8:12). I want to show you the relation between these two verses. Do you know what makes this dial shine in the dark? The radium itself. But it has to be exposed to the light before it will shine. It holds and reflects the light to which it has been exposed. Just so the Christian is to reflect the glory of the Lord.

Have you ever noticed, for instance, that just after you have turned off the light in the room the clock or watch will glow very brightly, and gradually become dimmer and dimmer, until sometimes, if it has been in the darkness long enough, you can't tell the time at all? When Christians, even boys and girls, haven't been with the Lord Jesus, who is the Light of the world, they don't shine forth for Him.

How can you be with the Lord? Through prayer and by reading His Word. If you do these things, you will reflect His glory so that others will be able to see it.

25

My Heart

OBJECT: Your own heart.

LESSON: Christ continuously intercedes for us (Hebrews 7:25).

PRESENTATION: Last night, boys and girls, as I was lying in bed, I began to think about this heart of mine. It's been beating regularly night and day for many years, and although I seldom stop to think about my heart, I'm extremely thankful that it keeps right on going whether or not I stop to think about it.

While I was thinking about my heart, my thoughts turned to something else that is going on just as regularly as the beating of my heart. Do you know what that is? It is the work that the Lord Jesus Christ is doing—praying for every Christian all the time. The Bible says that "he ever liveth to make intercession" (Hebrews 7:25), which simply means that the Lord Jesus is at the Father's right hand praying for you right now, and He is doing that all the time.

We will never know, boys and girls, how many temptations or trials did not come into our lives because the Lord Jesus was faithfully carrying on this ministry of prayer for us. Isn't it wonderful to have such a Saviour? But don't you think that we ought to thank Him for doing this for us? Someday this heart of mine will stop beating, but the Lord Jesus Christ will never stop praying for you. You often hear about people who have "heart failure," but the Lord never fails, and day after day and night after night He prays for you. Right now let's bow our heads and thank our Saviour for what He is doing.

26

An Onion

OBJECT: An onion or some perfume.

LESSON: Fellowship with the world shows.

PRESENTATION: I'm not going to show you the object right away. I have it here in my hand behind my back, and I think as soon as I let one of you smell my hand you will be able to tell me what the object is. Will one of you smell my hand? Now you know that the object is an onion.

We're going to learn a lesson from this onion. It represents all the wrong things that Christian boys and girls do. We'll sum them all up and call them "the things of the world." As soon as any of you Christian boys and girls comes in contact with any of the things of the world, then just as the smell of this onion comes off on my hands, so each sin with which you come in contact will come off on your lives.

Do you think that the Lord Jesus likes to have His children smelling like the things of the world? Of course not, but when you do these things, they surely will leave marks on your lives. Moreover, you are saying to the Lord that He cannot satisfy you, but that you prefer to fill up on the things of the world.

So remember, boys and girls, every time you taste of the things of the world, your Christian lives will show it. Onion stain will wash off, and Christ will cleanse your sins if you will confess them (1 John 1:9). If your lives are stained, confess your sins now, and then live a clean life for the Lord Jesus. Don't be an onion-stained Christian.

27

Fish, Salt, and You

OBJECT: A piece of cooked fish.

LESSON: "Ye are not of the world" (John 15:19).

PRESENTATION: The other night we had some fish to eat for supper, and I saved a piece of it to bring today because as I was eating it a truth I want to share with you came to my own heart. Now this is a sea fish, and it lived in the ocean all of its life. How many years, I do not know, but I do know that during its lifetime that fish got next to a lot of salt in the sea in which it lived. If you have ever tasted ocean water you know how salty it is, and you can easily imagine how much salt that fish must have absorbed.

But, when I took the first mouthful of this fish the other night, the first thing I said was, "Pass the salt." In spite of all the time that fish spent in the ocean it didn't seem to pick up a bit of salt. It wasn't any more salty than if it had lived all of its life in fresh water.

The lesson for those of us who are Christians is this: All of our life we live in this world. It is just as corrupt and sinful and wicked as Satan can make it. We hear foul talk, we see evil deeds, and we have to associate with corrupt men. Yet the Lord Jesus expects none of that to rub off on us, because we do not belong to this world. We are citizens of heaven. How are your life and testimony? Are they pure or defiled?

28

Salt

OBJECT: Some salt.

LESSON: "Ye are the salt of the earth" (Matthew 5:13).

PRESENTATION: Here's some salt. Christians are like salt, our Lord said. Just how are Christians like salt?

Well, what do you use salt for? You shake it on food in order to give the food a better flavor. Food is often blah without salt. Just so, our lives ought to attract people to Christ and make them want to have the same happiness we have. Of course, not everyone will be attracted, because some are so sinful that our Christian life is too convicting for them. That's like rubbing salt in a wound—it really stings.

Salt has another function which most of us don't know anything about. It's used to preserve things. Meat packers use it, and farmers preserve hay by adding salt to it. You know that salt kills germs, because you have probably used it to gargle or to clean your teeth. This preserving and cleansing power of salt is its principal use in the world even today.

And this is the principal meaning of the Lord's statement that we believers are the salt of the world. Our presence in the world keeps things from getting so corrupt. Christians don't participate in the evil things that other people do. For instance, you probably hear swearing at school, but you don't have to participate. You can help keep your school clean by the kind of language you don't use and the kind you do. You are the salt of your school. Paul wrote: "Let your speech be alway with grace, seasoned with salt" (Colossians 4:6).

Salt loses its sharpness if it is stored too long. Likewise, if you hide the fact that you are a Christian, you aren't much use to the Lord. So this week remember to do good things at home, school, everywhere, because you are the salt of the earth.

29

Keeping Warm

OBJECT: A soldering iron. (This lesson may also be based on a piece of ice.)

LESSON: Believers need to keep close to the Lord.

PRESENTATION: I don't suppose that many of you have ever used this object, but all of you know that it is a soldering iron, and I imagine that you have seen one used. We're going to let it represent everyone here who is a Christian—that is, everyone who has accepted the Lord Jesus Christ as his or her own personal Saviour.

In order to use this iron, it is necessary that it be hot, and I have to put it near the fire (*plug it in if it is electric*) so it will get warm. Just so, the Christian boy or girl who wants to be used by the Lord has to be warm. How does a Christian get warm? Not by being put into a fire, but rather, by being close to the Lord Jesus Christ. You boys and girls should talk to the Lord Jesus every day in prayer, and you must read the Bible so that you will be close to Him and He will be able to use you.

Notice that this iron is no good to me the way it is, and that is just as true of you if you are a cold Christian. Are you reading your Bible, and are you praying to the Lord regularly? The Lord wants to use each of you, but He can't if you are a cold Christian. So let's remember to be regular in doing these important things so that we won't be cold, useless Christians but warm, useful Christians for our Saviour.

30
Growing Up

OBJECT: Two children of different ages and sizes.

LESSON: We should grow in the Lord.

PRESENTATION: I didn't bring my objects with me today because I want two of you to come up here and be the objects. You see that these two children are of different sizes, and I want to show you why some people grow more in the Lord than others do.

First of all, how old are you? You see that these children are different ages. There are some people who have been saved longer than others, and for that reason they have grown more in the Christian life. But there's another reason why both of these children grew. From the time they were born, they have been eating every day. If you don't eat, you don't grow, and the more you eat, the more you grow. Remember that the same thing applies to the Christian life. The more you read the Bible, the more you will grow. If you never read the Bible, you can't expect to grow in the Christian life. Don't be a starved Christian.

But there's something else you must do if you expect to grow either physically or spiritually. If these children did nothing but eat, this alone would not make them grow: they must also exercise. Christians need to exercise, too—that is, they need to work for the Lord Jesus. "But," you say, "I don't know how to work for Jesus." Let me ask you how you learned to play baseball. After someone had explained the game, you had to get out on the field and try it for yourself and keep practicing. It's the same in the Lord's work. Even if you can't pray in public or tell others about the Lord, you have to keep doing it. I'll guarantee that the more you do it, the easier it will become, and the more you do these things, the faster you will grow as a Christian.

How much have you grown as a Christian? Maybe you have not started. Of course, you must be born before you can grow, and you must be born again before you can grow in the Lord. If any of you have never been born again, you can be right now if you will ask the Lord Jesus Christ to come into your hearts. He died for you; He wants to save you. Will you let Him?

31

A Piece of Bread

OBJECT: A piece of bread.

LESSON: Christ is the bread of life (John 6).

PRESENTATION: Look what I have today—just an ordinary piece of bread. In John 6 the Lord Jesus Christ likened Himself to bread. Why could Christ say, "I am the bread of life"? Well, bread is a necessary food, isn't it? Just so, Christ is necessary to everyone. Unsaved people need Christ in order to have eternal life. Saved people need Him every day. Most of you eat bread daily, I suppose, and you need to feed on Christ every day in order that your spiritual life may grow. You need to read your Bible every day, and you need to talk to the Lord in prayer.

Almost everybody eats and likes bread. It is suitable for all. Just so, the Lord Jesus Christ is suited for everybody. He can meet your every need no matter what it is. He can help you if you need salvation and eternal life, for He has said, "He that eateth of this bread shall live for ever" (John 6:58). He can help you if you are saved and need help, for God has said that He will supply all your need (Philippians 4:19). Bread is a satisfying food, and Christ, the Bread of life, satisfies every need.

Maybe some of you here have never tasted of Christ, the Bread of life. What's the first step in eating this bread? Yes, taking it into the mouth. And the first step you must take is to take Jesus Christ, not into your mouth, but into your heart. He said, "If any man hear my voice, and open the door, I will come in to him" (Revelation 3:20).

Will you bow your heads? If you boys and girls who are not saved will open your hearts and take the Bread of life, you will receive eternal life. Talk to the Lord Jesus about it right now.

32

A Loaf of Bread

OBJECT: A loaf of bread.

LESSON: Every Christian is a member of the body of Christ
(1 Corinthians 10:17).

PRESENTATION: In our last lesson, you remember, I used a piece
of bread to represent Christ, the Bread of life. Today you see I
I have a loaf of bread which represents the body of Christ. Why
is this a good object for our lesson? Because this loaf of bread is
one loaf and yet made up of many parts. That is true also of the
body of Christ. There is just one body, yet it is made up of
many parts. Those parts are you and I if you are saved. Only
those who have really believed in the Lord Jesus Christ are
members of His body.

Notice, too, boys and girls, that everyone who is saved is a
member of the body of Christ. This means that no matter what
church you belong to here on earth, or whether or not you are a
member of any church, if you really have Jesus Christ as your
own Saviour, then you are a member of His body. We have
many different churches and denominations, but there is only
one body of Christ. As Paul says, "For we being many are one
bread, and one body" (1 Corinthians 10:17). So don't look
down on someone who may belong to a different church, because
if that person is really saved, he is in the body of Christ just as
much as you are.

If you are not saved today, you can be right now by simply
accepting Jesus Christ as the One who died for your sins on the
cross. Then you, too, will be a member of His body.

33

Hypocrisy

OBJECT: A book with the jacket of a different book on it.

LESSON: Hypocrisy is trying to be something you are not.

PRESENTATION: Say, boys and girls, I want to show you a very good book I have been reading this week. Here it is. You can see by the jacket that it is a book of jungle stories. They're some of the most exciting I have ever read. Let me read part of one to you. Listen: "Take one teaspoon of sugar. . . ." What in the world is this? Why look. I don't have the jungle story book at all. This is a cook book. Somebody put the jacket of the story book on top of this cook book and fooled me into thinking this was the story book.

A big word will describe what I have just shown to you. The word is hypocrisy. You know the Lord Jesus had some very strong and condemning words to say about hypocrisy and hypocrites—about people who pretend to be one thing on the outside and are quite a different thing on the inside. Nobody likes a hypocrite—just as I did not like it at all when I found that this wasn't the book I thought it was. A hypocrite deceives people and leads them astray, because he says he is one thing and in reality he is entirely different.

Now do you see how this applies to Christians? Sometimes there are hypocrites who pretend to be saved but really are not. But more often hypocrites are found among Christian people who really do belong to the Lord Jesus but who are not living lives that show it. The Word of God says that we should lay aside all hypocrisies (1 Peter 2:1), because such action is very displeasing to our Lord. Will you ask the Lord to help you this week to live a true Christian life?

34

Like a Diamond

OBJECT: A diamond.

LESSON: "Let your light so shine before men, that they may see your good works, and glorify your Father which is in heaven" (Matthew 5:16).

PRESENTATION: There are a lot of things about a diamond that ought to be true of every Christian. The most obvious thing about a diamond is that it shines, and certainly that ought to be the chief characteristic of every Christian. A diamond does not have any light inside of itself, but it picks up outside light and reflects it back to your eye. That's the same way it is with a Christian. We are nothing of ourselves, but we reflect the beauties and glories of Jesus Christ, the light of the world.

You know, when a diamond comes out of the ground it doesn't look like this one bit. It's all dirty and it has to be cut and cleaned and polished before it can shine brilliantly. When the Lord saved you and me, He picked us up out of the dirt of sin, washed away all that sin, and polished us so we could shine for Him.

What would you think of a person who had a diamond but who kept it in his dresser drawer, or kept it hidden in a closet? You would think he was ashamed or afraid, wouldn't you? What do you think of a Christian who has Jesus Christ in his heart and who never lets anyone know about the Lord? You would think the same thing—either that person was ashamed of Jesus or afraid to tell others about Him. What do you think the Lord thinks about such a person? Listen, if you are a Christian, are you really shining for Him at home, in school, and everywhere? What does the Lord think of you today?

35

Special Delivery

OBJECT: A special delivery letter or simply a special delivery stamp.

LESSON: God's message is urgent.

PRESENTATION: Look, boys and girls, what I received this week—a special delivery letter. In fact, it came by airmail to speed it to the city and then special delivery to speed it to my house. You know, of course, why it came special delivery—the message inside was urgent and had to get to me as quickly as possible.

The Bible is God's message to all the world, and He wants us to deliver it. Unsaved friends of yours urgently need to hear that Christ died for their sins, and Christians need to know how God wants them to live. Paul tells us that "now is the day of salvation" (2 Corinthians 6:2); we need to bring this message to people special delivery. You can do this now by being witnesses for Christ at school and at home. Later when you grow up, some of you may be given the privilege of being missionaries to deliver God's Word to people in foreign lands.

How much does it cost to send a letter by regular mail? And how long does it take to be delivered? Well, I imagine if this letter had come by regular mail from Ohio, it would have taken about four or five days. If you put an airmail stamp on it, it costs more, but the letter is apt to arrive in two or three days. Special delivery, which costs a great deal more, brought this letter to me in twenty-four hours! So if I see a lot of postage on a letter, I know that there must be something very important inside.

It cost God the death of His Son to make possible His sending us the message of salvation. The importance of the gospel can be measured by its cost, which was the death of Jesus Christ. And it's this gospel which we've been given the privilege of delivering to the world.

36

Fifth-Amendment Christians

OBJECT: A copy of the fifth amendment of the Constitution of the United States of America.

LESSON: Christians should witness for Christ.

PRESENTATION: We're hearing a lot these days about the fifth amendment to the Constitution, because some people are hiding behind it when they're called upon to tell certain things about themselves. Some of you have read or heard your folks talk about the Communists who were investigated by Congress and who refused to tell whether or not they ever were Communists. Now the reason they had a right to refuse to tell is that the fifth amendment to the Constitution says that a man shall not "be compelled in any criminal case to be a witness against himself." And these people know, of course, that if they admit that they are Communists, they will get into trouble, so they hide behind this amendment.

Personally, I have very little patience with such people, but I'm afraid that a lot of Christians act just the same way about their Christianity. They're afraid that if they let people know they are Christians, they will get into trouble, so they refuse to speak for Christ or even act like a Christian should. They're hiding behind the fact that you can get away without witnessing for the Lord and still be a Christian. But what kind of a Christian is such a person? You know perfectly well that your school chums are always asking whether you are a Christian by the way they watch your life to see if it's any different from their own. How are you answering them? Don't be a fifth-amendment Christian. Let the whole world know where you stand.

37

The Finished Product

OBJECT: A book.

LESSON: Each Christian should do his part in the Lord's work.

PRESENTATION: I brought along a book this morning. Because it's something you use every day, it will be easy to remember the lesson. This is the best book that I've ever seen. Isn't it nice looking? Look at that jacket. Of course, I may be a little prejudiced because I wrote it, but I do think it's a very good-looking book. Now I want to use this book to remind you of some things about our Sunday school (or church). This is your church, and you ought to be just as interested in your own church as I am in my own book. It's yours, and there's not one better.

Think a minute of all that went into this book. All I did was to write it. Then the postman took the manuscript to the publisher, and some people in his office checked it to see that I didn't misspell any words and put it into proper form. Then it was sent to the printer and to the binder. Of course someone cut the trees and others helped make the paper it was printed on. Too, someone was drawing the design for the jacket and composing the jacket blurb. Finally, when all the jobs were done, the book was produced—a finished product.

Now the point is that it takes a lot of people to make a Sunday school or church service successful. Someone has to prepare the lessons or sermons. That's like writing the book. Some sing in the choir; some usher; some lead in prayer. Someone has to tell others about the service just as someone has to sell my book. It doesn't do any good to have thousands of copies of this book stacked in some warehouse, does it? Perhaps your job is to bring someone to church. All of us have to pray, for without prayer we cannot function. Tomorrow morning when you pick up your books at school, will you remember to pray for Sunday school next Sunday?

38

Tearing Down or Building Up?

OBJECT: A rose in bloom.

LESSON: A Christian should not tear things or people down (Philippians 4:8).

PRESENTATION: I need someone to help me with the object lesson today. All right, you come up and help me. Do you see this rose? Now, I'm going to take my watch off and time you while you do something. I want you to pick all the petals off the rose one at a time, and we'll see how long it takes you. All right, ready, go.

That took exactly twenty-one seconds. Very good. Now I want to time you while you do something else. This time I want you to put all the petals back on. Ready? Go. What's the matter? You can't do it?

Now, boys and girls, this is the lesson I want you to remember today. It's always much easier to tear down than to build up. I'm speaking to you who belong to the Lord because a lot of Christians have never learned this lesson. They go around thinking the meanest things they can and saying the most unkind words to others, and in every way they tear down the character of other people. A Christian shouldn't act that way. His mind, mouth, and manner should always be filled with things that build up. Listen to this verse from Philippians 4: "Finally, brethren, whatsoever things are true, whatsoever things are honest, whatsoever things are just, whatsoever things are pure, whatsoever things are lovely, whatsoever things are of good report; if there be any virtue, and if there be any praise, think on these things" (v. 8). Does that sound like tearing down or like building up?

Remember this lesson this week, and when you're tempted to say or even think something that is not nice or right, ask the Lord to help you put that thought out of your mind.

39

Filled and Used

OBJECT: A fountain pen which has no ink in it.

LESSON: A Christian has to be filled with the Spirit to be used of the Lord.

PRESENTATION: Have you ever thought about how a fountain pen resembles a Christian? Just think about it a moment. Look at my pen here. It's a very good one; indeed, I would say it is just about perfect. It has a good point, it never leaks, it always fills properly, in every way I find it perfect. When God saved you, He made you perfect in His sight.

However, if you are going to be useful for the Lord, something else is necessary. Let me show you what I mean by trying to write something with this pen. Well, what do you know, it won't write. I wonder what's the matter. Why, there's no ink in it. It's not filled. Now, boys and girls, the same thing is true in the Christian life. You won't be useful to the Lord unless you are filled with His strength, His power, His wisdom, by being filled with His Holy Spirit (Ephesians 5:18). How can you be filled with the Holy Spirit? By being sure there is no sin in your life that you haven't confessed to the Lord.

Can this pen write by itself? Of course not. I have to hold it and use it. And that's the way it is in the Christian life. God has to have control of your life in order to be able to use it. You can't do it yourself, but God can do limitless things with your life if you will let Him. If you've never told the Lord that He can have complete control of you, won't you do that today?

40

Strength in Unity

OBJECT: A piece of paper and a large book like a telephone book.

LESSON: Why we should join a church.

PRESENTATION: A lot of you boys and girls are Christians, aren't you? You already have accepted Jesus as your Saviour from sin, and you know for sure that He has come into your heart. That's the most wonderful thing in the world, and it makes you sure that some day the Lord Jesus will take you to be with Him in heaven. But, in the meantime, you have a life to live on earth, and you want to live it for His glory.

One thing that will help you in this life is to associate yourself after you are saved with other Christians by joining a church. Now we don't join a church because we think the Lord works only through churches, but because we find strength and help for our lives from other Christians. After all, a church is not a building; it is a group of people who have trusted Christ as their Saviour and who are organized to carry on His work. A group of people joined together in this way can carry on the work better than if each tried to do it himself.

Look at this piece of paper. Is there anybody in the room today who couldn't tear it in half? Of course not. That's very easy to do. Now look at this telephone book. Is there anyone here who can tear this in half? I doubt it. Look how difficult it is to tear. Do you know the reason? It's simple, isn't it? When you put together a number of sheets of paper, each of which is easy to tear, you cannot tear them when they are bound together. And that's an illustration of what I've been talking about today. Alone, you can do a lot for the Lord, and it certainly is important that you do all you can do individually for Him every day, but often together we can do more. Also when we're together it's more difficult for Satan to attack us and tear us apart. You should belong to a church, and you should attend, support, and work for that church. God says we must not forsake the assembling of ourselves together (Hebrews 10:25).

41

Light Bulbs

OBJECT: Several light bulbs of different sizes.

LESSON: The witness of every Christian is important.

PRESENTATION: I wonder if you ever felt that it wasn't very important whether or not you witnessed for the Lord. "After all," you may have said, "I'm just one person," or "I'm too young and small," or "What can I do to lead others to Jesus?" Now look at this light bulb. It's a big 150 watt one. There's no question about how important this bulb is or what a big light it furnishes.

Now look at this one. It's just a 60 watt one. Well, you say, now you're getting down to my size. All right, have you ever stopped to count how many bulbs of this size you have in use at home? You probably have just one or two big ones, but perhaps a dozen or more smaller ones. They are rather necessary, aren't they? Now look at this tiny one. It's a night light. Not very big, but very important if the whole house is dark except for this one light. Suppose this little light said, "I'm not very important. Folks can get along without me. I don't think I'll shine at all."

Do you see the point? Maybe you are not a big preacher. That's all right. God may make you one some day. But even if you're only a night light, your faithful witness, even though you think it isn't very strong or big, might mean the difference between the salvation or the fall of some soul. Wouldn't you like to ask the Lord right now to help you be a good testimony for Him everywhere you go this week?

42

Walking

OBJECT: You.

LESSON: The Christian life is a walk of faith.

PRESENTATION: Did you know, boys and girls, that every day you do something which God uses as an illustration of the Christian life? That something is walking, for our whole Christian life is called a walk. As a matter of fact it is called a walk of faith (2 Corinthians 5:7), which is just the same as saying a walk, or life, which is in total dependence on God and His power.

Have you ever analyzed your process of walking? Well, let's do that today. Look at me now. When I want to walk I simply place one foot in front of the other, but every time I do that I am putting all my faith on the foot that is not in the air to hold me up. You see, when I lift my right foot I am trusting my left one to hold me until the right one reaches the floor again. Every time I take a step, I do it in faith that the one foot will hold me. Walking is an act of faith.

The Christian life is also of faith, and the Lord Jesus wants you to live your life depending on Him. If you're tempted to lose your temper, why not try depending on Him to help you control it? If you need help in telling others about Jesus, why not depend on Him for it? That's what faith is—dependence on someone or something else. And the Christian life is a life of dependence.

Try it this week, will you? Walk by faith in your risen Lord.

43

The Temperature

OBJECT: A thermometer.

LESSON: How to take your spiritual temperature.

PRESENTATION: How would you like to have your temperature taken today? Not your physical temperature but your spiritual temperature. I want to see if any of you are sick. All right, open your mouths, and I'll put the thermometer in by asking you a few questions.

First of all, did you read your Bible every day this past week? Of course, if your daddy or mother read it to you in a family group you may answer yes to the question. If you didn't read it every day, then answer with the number of days you did read it.

Second, did you pray to the Lord regularly every day this past week? Again, if you have family devotions you may answer yes to the question. Actually, however, all of you are about old enough now to pray by yourselves too even if you do have family devotions also.

Third, what about your life this week? Did you try to live the way a Christian boy or girl should? When you had a chance to speak a word for the Lord, did you do it? This will be a very hard question to score, but I think you know well enough what a Christian ought to be like to be able to answer correctly. Be honest now.

What's your grade on this little quiz? Is it anywhere near 100? It ought to be. You know, even the temperature of your body to be normal should be nearly 100. Maybe someone is saying, "What difference does it make? I won't die spiritually if my temperature isn't normal." That's true, for if you are really saved, you are saved eternally. But listen while I read to you what God thinks about Christians whose temperature is below normal. (*Read Revelation 3:16*). Just as you don't like a lukewarm drink of water, God can't stand a lukewarm Christian. Maybe we ought to check our temperature a little more often. Suppose you watch yours this week as you try to live for the Lord.

44

The Importance of Today

OBJECT: A match.

LESSON: Make every day count for Christ.

PRESENTATION: Well, another week has gone by, hasn't it? Seven whole days since we last met together. Do you think you will ever live last week over again? Why, of course not. You will never have another chance to live any day over again, because once it's gone, it's gone forever.

Look at this match. First I'll strike it, and then I'll let it burn for a few seconds like this. Now I think it has burned enough so I will blow it out. Now suppose I say to the match, "Get unburned!" Isn't that silly? The match cannot possibly replace the part that has already burned, can it? I'll never be able to strike this match again or burn the part that is already burned.

But now I'm awfully sorry that I struck it. I wish I had waited until tomorrow. Is my sorrow going to replace the match? Of course not. Well, I'll refuse to think that the match is actually burned. Is refusing to think about it going to change the fact that it is burned? Certainly not. You see, it's done, and there's absolutely nothing I can do about it. I should have thought of all these things before I struck the match.

Life is like that match. Once a day is over, you cannot live it again. Do you see how important it is for you who are Christians to live for the Lord Jesus every day? Being sorry for mistakes may teach you a lesson, but it won't let you live the time over. Refusing to think about what has happened will not change history. You know, you ought to form the habit of asking the Lord every morning to help you to make that day count for Him—a day in which you will have no regrets for the way that you have lived. He will help you.

45

Heaven

OBJECT: A photograph of some well-known place.

LESSON: What heaven is like.

PRESENTATION: I wonder if anyone recognizes the picture I am holding up right now. Yes, it's a picture of the Grand Canyon. How many of you have ever been to the Grand Canyon? Well, if you have not, then the next best thing is to look at pictures of it, isn't it?

How many of you have ever been to heaven? No one? Well, how many of you have seen a picture of heaven? No one? No, as far as I know, no one has ever taken a photograph of heaven. But someone did see heaven and came back to earth to give us a word picture of it. Do you know who? Well, it was the apostle John. His detailed word picture of heaven is recorded in the last two chapters of the Bible. Let me read to you some of the things he says about heaven. (*Read Revelation 21:1-4, 21; 22: 1-5*).

Doesn't that sound like the most wonderful place you have ever heard of? I wonder how many of you are absolutely sure that you will some day see that place John described? You can be sure, for John tells us who is going to be in heaven. (Read Revelation 21:27.) All of those and only those whose names are written in the Lamb's book of life will be in heaven. Who are those people? Why, they are the Christians, those who have believed on Christ as their Saviour. They will populate heaven. You may ask, "How can I belong to that group?" Not by joining this church, for no church has possession of the book of life. Not by baptism, for water won't write your name in that book. But by accepting the Lord Jesus Christ into your heart as your Saviour from sin, you can be assured that you belong to the group that will be in heaven.

46

A Flashlight

OBJECT: A flashlight.

LESSON: "Thy word is a lamp unto my feet, and a light unto my path" (Psalm 119:105).

PRESENTATION: Have you ever been outdoors late at night when it is very very dark and you can hardly see your hand in front of your face? If you have, you know how handy a flashlight is under such circumstances. Does anyone remember a verse in the Bible that tells us that God's Word is like a lamp to guide us through the darkness of sin? Yes, it's Psalm 119:105. Let's say it together.

What does a flashlight do for you in the darkness? Well, for one thing, it keeps you from tripping over something in the path. Just so the Word of God if hidden in your heart will keep you from stumbling or sinning in your Christian life (Psalm 119: 11). The Word of God tells us how we should talk and act, and where we should go. If we use it to guide us, we won't sin. A good flashlight will show you where you are going by shining its beam ahead of you. And God's Word does the same thing for a Christian.

Are you using God's light, His Word, every day, to show you how to live in this dark world? You have to turn a flashlight on for it to be of use, and likewise you have to read and study the Bible for it to be of any use. Will you promise God you will read it every day this week?

47

A Compass

OBJECT: A compass.

LESSON: The Word of God is our guide.

PRESENTATION: How many of you know what this is? How many have ever used a compass before? If you have, you know that it can be very useful, especially if you are lost.

You know, the Word of God is like a compass because it's a guide for our lives. When you hold the compass level, it points to the north, therefore, you can tell in which direction you are headed. That's exactly what the Bible does, too, boys and girls. It points to God, to Christ, to heaven, to right living now. As you read it you can tell which direction you are heading. If the Lord Jesus is not your Saviour, then God's compass says that you are heading in the direction of hell. If you are a Christian and you are lying, cheating, gossiping, or disobeying your parents, God's Word says that you are not headed in the direction of right Christian living.

Once in a while a compass will not point north. That happens when a lot of metal is near, which tends to pull the needle away from the magnetic pole. There's nothing wrong with the compass itself—it's just that something has come between it and the north pole. Sometimes people can misinterpret the Word of God, too. It's not that the Word is wrong or has changed its meaning. But, sin has come between God and the person who is reading it, and that sin may cause you to think you are going in the right direction when you really are not. In such a case you must correct the thing that is causing the deviation by confessing your sin to the Lord.

Remember, God's Word is always true, but in order to understand it aright, you must not have unconfessed sin in your life when you read it. Then if you read it and live by it, you will be guided unerringly into right paths—into God's paths.

48

My Glasses

OBJECT: A pair of glasses.

LESSON: We need the teaching of the Holy Spirit (John 16:13).

PRESENTATION: Today I am going to use my own glasses as the object. (*A pair may be borrowed, but they should have optical lenses.*) We are going to let these glasses represent the Holy Spirit. Do you know why I have to wear glasses? Simply because I need them in order to see clearly. Do you know what important ministry the Holy Spirit is carrying on today? He is here living inside every Christian to help him understand what the Bible says. Listen to this verse, "Howbeit when he, the Spirit of truth, is come, he will guide you into all truth" (John 16:13). Just as I cannot see without my glasses, so you cannot understand the truths of the Bible without the Holy Spirit.

Wouldn't I be foolish to leave these glasses at home in my dresser drawer when I know that I need them? And yet that is exactly what many Christians do with regard to the teaching ministry of the Holy Spirit—they never avail themselves of His wonderful work.

You know that these glasses were made especially for me, and they aren't much help to anyone else. Any change in my eyes would mean that I would have to get new glasses. So the Holy Spirit works in your heart to meet your special need, whatever it may be. If I may reverently say so, He is for everyone of you a special pair of glasses to help you see and understand the things that are in God's Word. Isn't it wonderful that God has given us this help? If you have trusted the Lord Jesus as your Saviour, then the Holy Spirit lives in you, and if you will let Him, He will help you to understand the Bible.

49

Ask the Author

OBJECT: A note that you have written to someone in the audience.

LESSON: The Holy Spirit has been sent to teach us the meaning of the Bible (John 16:13-15).

PRESENTATION: *Let the person to whom you wrote the note come to the front with it and carry on with you a conversation similar to the following.*

PUPIL: There's something in this note you wrote me that I don't quite understand.

TEACHER: All right, I will tell you what it means. What is it that you don't understand?

PUPIL: It's this sentence right here.

TEACHER: Well, it means this. . . . Do you understand now?

PUPIL: Yes, thank you very much.

TEACHER: Tell me, why did you come to me and ask about this note? Why didn't you ask one of your friends?

PUPIL: Actually I did ask someone else if they understood what you meant, but since he didn't know, I thought I'd better ask you. After all, you're the one who wrote it, and of all people you should know what you mean.

TEACHER: You're quite right. There's no better person you could have asked than me, since I was the author of this note.

Boys and girls, who wrote the Bible? Yes, a lot of men, but all of them under the direction of the Holy Spirit (2 Peter 1:21), so actually the Holy Spirit is the author. Jesus said before He left the earth that He would send the Holy Spirit to help every Christian to understand the Bible (John 16:13-15). Since the Holy Spirit lives in every Christian, you can go to Him at any time. So as you read your Bible, ask Him to help you understand what you're reading.

50

A Mirror

OBJECT: A small mirror.

LESSON: It is important to read the Old Testament (1 Corinthians 10:11).

PRESENTATION: You all know what this object is, don't you? Yes, it's a small mirror. Why do you use a mirror? Well, sometimes you use it to look at yourself in order to see if your hair is combed or your face is clean. But there's another use for a mirror that I want you to think about today. Sometimes you use a mirror in order to see what is behind you. The best example of this use is the mirror in your automobile.

For the same reason, boys and girls, the Bible records many of the stories in the Old Testament. God wants us to know how He dealt with His people in former days so that we may know how He will deal with us today. The New Testament says that these things happened in former days as examples to us who are living today (1 Corinthians 10:11). For instance, you can tell from Old Testament stories what will happen when a Christian marries an unsaved person, for just as Israel always had trouble when she mixed with foreigners, so you will have difficulty if you marry an unsaved person. You also can tell from the Old Testament what God thinks of worshiping idols (Exodus 32).

What would you do if you were driving along in a car and saw a reckless driver bumping cars? Why you'd get out of the way. Just so, if you read in the Old Testament how Satan attacked men, you will be warned so it won't happen to you. But, if you're going to be warned, you have to read the Old Testament and learn from the experiences the people had in those days. So whenever you hear or read these accounts in the Old Testament ask the Lord to help you to learn the lesson He was trying to teach them, so that you will not make the same mistakes they did.

51

Stopped Watches

OBJECT: A watch of any kind that has stopped.

LESSON: A Christian needs to read his Bible continually (1 Peter 2:2).

PRESENTATION: Here is a watch, and it's a very good watch, but I have to do something to it every day. Yes, I have to wind it, and I have to do so every day if I want my watch to keep running.

We're going to let this watch represent every Christian, and what is accomplished by winding the watch is accomplished in the Christian's life by reading the Bible. Just as the watch needs winding every day, so we need to read the Bible every day. If I forget to wind this watch, it stops, and that's exactly what has happened to every one of you who knows the Lord Jesus as Saviour but who has stopped reading the Bible. You've stopped growing.

You can see that this watch has stopped, and it's no good to me this way, is it? Just so, a Christian who has stopped growing is not much help to the Lord; and just as you can plainly see that this watch has stopped, so other people can see when you stop feeding upon God's Word.

Perhaps some of you have been stopped—maybe for a long time. What are you going to do about it? If I want this watch to start going again, what do I have to do? Simply wind it, of course. And that's all you have to do if you want to start going places for the Lord Jesus again—simply start to read the Bible regularly again. Let's be faithful in this important matter.

52

Worship

OBJECT: A ten- or twenty-dollar bill.

LESSON: Worship is recognizing God's worth.

PRESENTATION: Do you know what the word *worship* means? We talk about going to the worship service, or having a worship experience, or being in an atmosphere of worship. What is worship? It is acknowledging the worth of something or someone. The old English word used to be spelled worthship, and then the *th* was dropped to make it *worship*. Worship is recognizing worth.

Here's a twenty-dollar bill. What's it worth? It's worth is a nice coat or several pairs of shoes or six or more admissions to ball games. When you were a little younger, you didn't know the difference between one dollar and twenty dollars. Mother and Dad bought all the things you needed, and money was unimportant in your life. But when you began to want things and realized how much money it took to buy them, then money began to mean something to you. You recognized the worth of money by what it could do for you.

God wants us to worship Him (John 4:24). That means that He wants us to recognize His worth. And what will help us to worship better? Knowing more about His worth by knowing what He can do.

When our children were growing up, we never took a twenty-dollar bill, framed it, put it on the wall and said, "Now children, worship!" As they learned what money could do, they respected its worth. Worship isn't really helped by putting a picture of Christ on the wall to look at. It is helped as we learn through experience what Christ can do. When He answers your prayers, when He helps you through temptation, then you realize how great He is, and that's worship. If you're not a Christian, remember His death on the cross was worth the payment for your sins. Receive Him today and be saved.

53

Time Is Running Out

OBJECT: A timer such as you might have around the kitchen.

LESSON: Christ is coming soon (Matthew 24:33).

PRESENTATION: Have you ever seen Mother use a timer like this when she's boiling eggs or baking a cake? Or perhaps you've used it to time a long-distance phone call. And if so, you remember that when the bell is almost ready to ring or the sand has almost gone all the way through the glass, you quickly finished up everything you had to say and got ready to hang up. Or sometimes Mother would open the oven and look at the cake and say, "It's almost done!" Then the timer would go off.

You know, this world is running according to God's timetable, and we are very near one of the most important events in all time. I'm talking about the return of the Lord Jesus to take believers to heaven to be with Him forever (1 Thessalonians 4:13-18). When this great event happens, believers who have died will be raised from their graves, and believers who are living will be changed in an instant and given new bodies.

What difference should it make that Christ's coming may be very near? Well, we don't quit what we're doing and sit out in some field waiting for Him! We make sure that each day we live a life that is pleasing to Him. Then whether He comes today or tomorrow or the next day, we'll be ready and anxious to see Him.

54

Water, Water Everywhere

OBJECT: A glass of water.

LESSON: The Noahic flood was very forceful.

PRESENTATION: I want one of you big, strong, he-man boys to volunteer to help me today with the object lesson. All I want you to do is to hold this glass of water for a little while. Only I want you to hold your arm stiff and straight out to your side while you're holding the glass. Easy, isn't it? At least right now it is. But just keep holding it.

That's just a little glass of water he's holding. Can you imagine how much water there was on the earth during the flood in Noah's day? It rained for forty days, but the water was on the earth an entire year, and during the flood water came from above and from below (Genesis 7:10-11). You remember, too, that the water covered Mount Ararat, which today is 17,260 feet above sea level. That's a lot of water. How's your arm feeling holding just a glass of water?

Water weighs something, doesn't it? I imagine many of you have carried a bucket of water to wash the car or something. A bucket full of water is a lot heavier than an empty bucket, isn't it? Can you imagine how much weight was dumped on the earth when the flood came? We know that everything that wasn't in the ark died, but what do you suppose happened to the bodies of people and animals that died? With all the upheaval of the earth and rocks and mountains and with all the weight of the water, they must have been pressed in the rocks. The traces and remains of these animals are the fossils which are found everywhere, and they are the result of this tremendous pressure that the water of the flood created on the earth.

How does your arm feel now? Ready to put the glass down? Even today about seventy percent of the surface of the earth is water, and it is Jesus Christ who is "upholding all things by the word of his power" (Hebrews 1:3).

55

Mind Your Mind

OBJECT: A real or toy hard hat such as construction workers use.

LESSON: We need to guard our minds.

PRESENTATION: Have you ever walked by a large construction job? If you have, you probably noticed that the men working all wore a hard hat like the one that I have here today. Too, there were signs posted around the site which said, "Do not enter unless wearing hard hat." Workers have to wear these hats to protect their heads from injury. They don't wear steel vests or iron pants, but they do wear hard hats.

God, too, recognizes the importance of protecting the head. When Paul describes the armor which the Christian wears, he speaks of the helmet of salvation (Ephesians 6:17). You see, we aren't saved just from the neck down. Salvation affects our minds also, for after we are saved we have new thoughts, new ideas, new outlooks. But the devil is powerful, and that's why we need to keep protecting our minds all the time with the helmet of salvation.

What would happen if a brick fell on a man who was wearing a hard hat? Nothing, and he would just go on working. Likewise, if your mind is always set on doing the will of God, then Satan's attacks won't hurt you a bit. You'll just go on living for the Lord. Paul put it this way: "Be ye transformed by the renewing of your mind, that ye may prove what is that good, and acceptable, and perfect, will of God" (Romans 12:2).

The mind controls the body, so it's important to keep your mind on the right things. Don't let impure thoughts in, because they may result in impure actions. Don't think evil things. Think on what is good (Philippians 4:8). Try minding your mind this week.

56

On Growing Up

OBJECT: Any kind of seed.

LESSON: "Whatsoever a man soweth, that shall he also reap" (Galatians 6:7).

PRESENTATION: It's springtime again, and in the spring people begin to think about planting grass or flowers or gardens. So I thought we might learn a lesson today from these few seeds that I brought along. You know, the Bible talks about sowing seed—that is like your life—when it warns that whatever you sow you will reap. If I sow this corn, which is what I have in my hand, then I don't expect to get tomatoes, do I? The same principle works in your life. If you sow little lies, you will reap big lies and lots of trouble with them. If you continue to refuse to accept Christ as your Saviour, you may grow up and never receive Him. If as a Christian boy or girl you sow irreverence in God's house by little whispers, you may reap a disregard for even attending services in God's house. When you sow evil you reap evil, and when you sow good things you will reap a good character.

"But," you may be saying, "any wrong thing I do now is awfully little and really can't amount to much." Look at this seed. Just a little thing, isn't it? But when it is planted, it will grow into a very large stalk of corn. Yes, the little sins you are doing now will grow into big sins in later years, and the good things you do, even though they seem very small and unimportant, are very important because they will reap for you a life well-pleasing to God. You see, it is extremely important that you pay careful attention to all the details of your everyday life. What you are now is what you will become when you grow up.

What kind of seeds are you sowing?

57

Joined Together

OBJECT: Several pieces of a jigsaw puzzle, including two pieces that fit together.

LESSON: Be preparing now for a good marriage.

PRESENTATION: Look at all these pieces of this jigsaw juzzle! How will I ever put them together? How many of you have ever worked a jigsaw puzzle? It's hard, isn't it? But remember how delighted you were when you found pieces that fit? "Here's the one!" "This one fits!" And you joined the pieces together into one beautiful picture.

You know, when the Lord Jesus talked about marriage, He said that a man and a woman should be joined together to fit perfectly just like those pieces of the puzzle. That's what the word "cleave" means in Matthew 19:5. When a man marries, he is joined to the woman he marries so that the two become one, so close is the union.

Now I know that some of you couldn't care less about marriage right now. But you will be before very long! May I suggest some things you should be doing now so that when you find the right one you will have a good, solid, happy marriage?

First, once in a while ask the Lord to guide you in this matter of marriage, even though it may seem a long way off now. From among all the people in the world, you want God to lead you to the right partner. Second, remember that you can never fit one piece from one jigsaw puzzle with any piece from a different puzzle. It just won't work. Likewise, you cannot even think about marrying someone who is not a Christian, because it won't work. And finally, keep yourself pure and your ideals high, and wait for God's time and choice. Then your marriage will fit together as it ought.

58

My Aching Foot

OBJECT: A small pebble.

LESSON: The Bible teaches truths about dating and marriage.

PRESENTATION: It's a wonderful thing to have friends, isn't it? God is interested in friendship so much that some day He wants you to find someone who will mean so much to you that you will want to marry that one and live together the rest of your lives. Naturally, then, God is interested also in the friends you have now and the boys and girls some of our older young people are dating right now. He's so interested in fact that He has taken the trouble to tell you some things about these relations with each other in His Word.

For one thing, God does not approve of marriage between a Christian and one who is not a Christian (2 Corinthians 6:14). Make no mistake about it, such a marriage will not work. You should have unsaved friends in order that you may win them to Christ, but not with any thought of marrying one. "Well," you say, "that really doesn't make too much difference, does it? After all we get along so well in everything else, and on Sundays we'll each go our own way." The fact that you are of differing religious faiths may not seem much to you now, but believe me, it will become a very big problem later on. Let me illustrate.

Look at this tiny pebble. You wouldn't think it could cause any trouble. Let me put it in my shoes like this. Why, I hardly feel it. Look, I can walk clear across the room and it doesn't even bother me. But, how do you suppose my foot will feel tonight if I leave this in all day? You're quite right, I'll certainly have a sore foot. A little thing can be very annoying after a long time.

Now do you get the point? Little differences in friendship may not seem important now, but when you walk through life with that little thing, it can become very annoying. Just be sure that God is leading you in all your dates and you won't need to worry, because He makes no mistakes.

59

On Communion Sunday

OBJECT: A letter.

LESSON: What communion means (1 Corinthians 11:24).

PRESENTATION: I think most of you boys and girls realize that today is Communion Sunday, a day on which we remember the Lord by observing the Lord's Supper. Even though some of you may be too young to participate in it, I want to talk to you a little today about its meaning and why we do it.

If you ever leave home to go to camp or school, one of the last things your mother will say to you is, "Don't forget to write." And of course you won't forget to write because you love your mother and you'll be thinking about her and how much you miss her. When the Lord Jesus went away to heaven, He asked His disciples to remember Him, not by writing letters but by observing the Lord's Supper together. And of course we do it because we love Him, we miss Him, and we like to sit down together around the communion table and think about Him and what He's done for us.

He Himself said that the bread which we eat represents His body which was broken on Calvary because of our sin, and the cup represents His blood which was shed when He died for our sins.

But perhaps all of this doesn't mean anything to you. Is it because Jesus doesn't mean anything to you? Why don't you take a good look at what He has done about sin in dying on the cross for you, and then tell Him you realize He died for you and you want Him to come into your heart. He will come in and take away all your sin right now, today. "For the Son of man is come to seek and to save that which was lost" (Luke 19:10).

60

On Easter

OBJECT: An Easter lily.

LESSON: Looking at God's provision of a Saviour is important.

PRESENTATION: Happy Easter! This is a grand day for all of us, isn't it? This is the day when people get out their new clothes and show them off to everybody. I won't ask how many of you have new clothes, because I can see that a lot of you have something new on today. This is also the day when we decorate our churches and homes with lilies. Here is one I brought today.

You know, we learn a lesson about clothes from lilies. The Lord Himself taught the lesson. He said that we ought to consider or think about the lily, because it is so much more beautiful than any clothes any man can wear. His point was that we ought not to be thinking about clothes and food and all the things of life because God can provide them for us as much as we need, and the proof that He can provide is how beautifully He made the lily. Have you ever seen an Easter outfit as beautiful and perfect as this lily?

It's nice to be dressed up, but the Lord wants us to be thinking about Him and all the things He can and will do for us. There's no better time to think about Him than on Easter, for Easter reminds us of the greatest thing the Lord ever did or will do for man. It reminds us that He died for our sins, and that He rose from the dead to take away sin. The greatest thing on Easter is not a new suit or even a pretty lily. The greatest thing on Easter is to have the gift of a Saviour in your own heart. Is Jesus in your heart today? If not, why not ask Him to come in and take away all your sins. He will, for He promised that He would (Revelation 3:20).